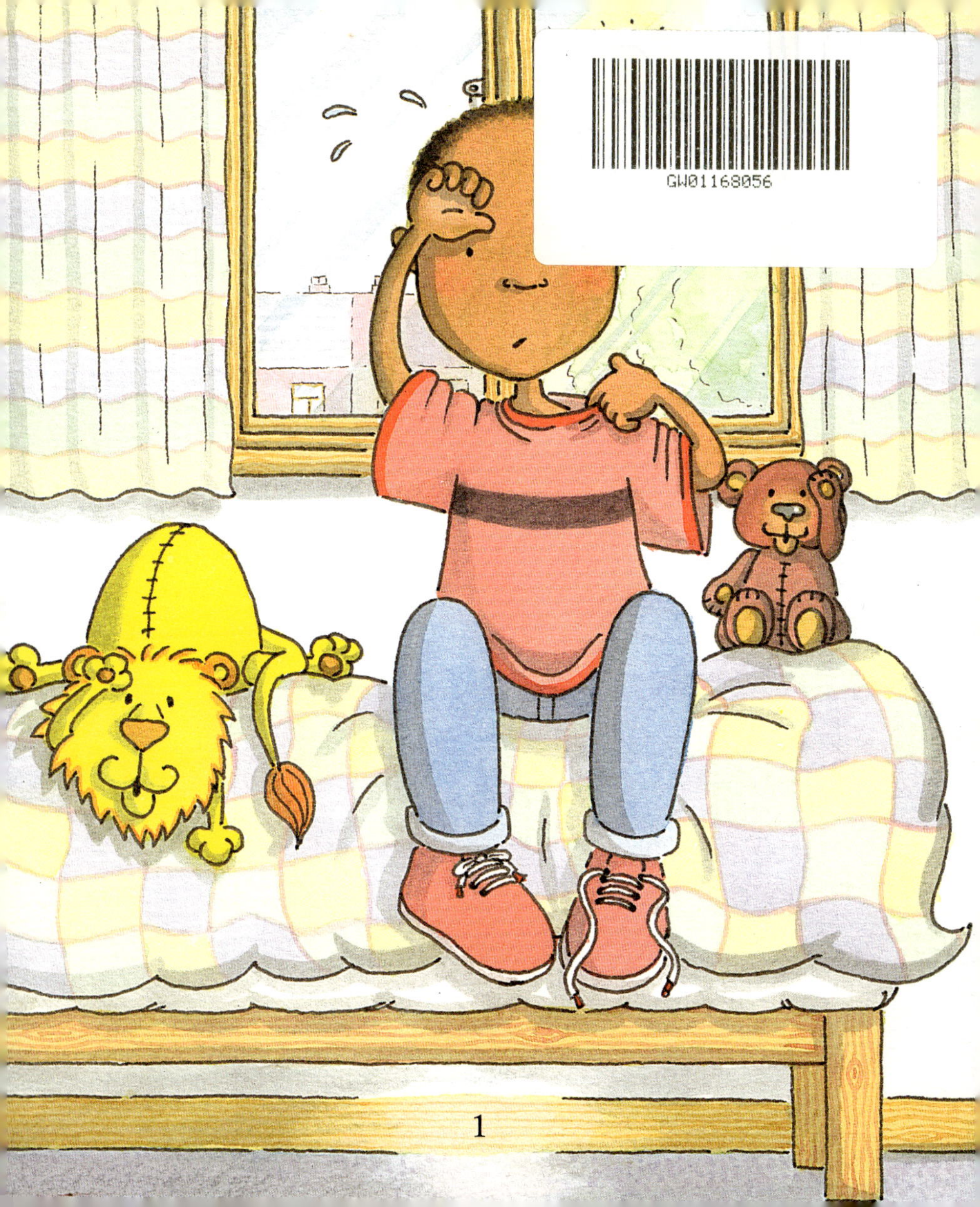

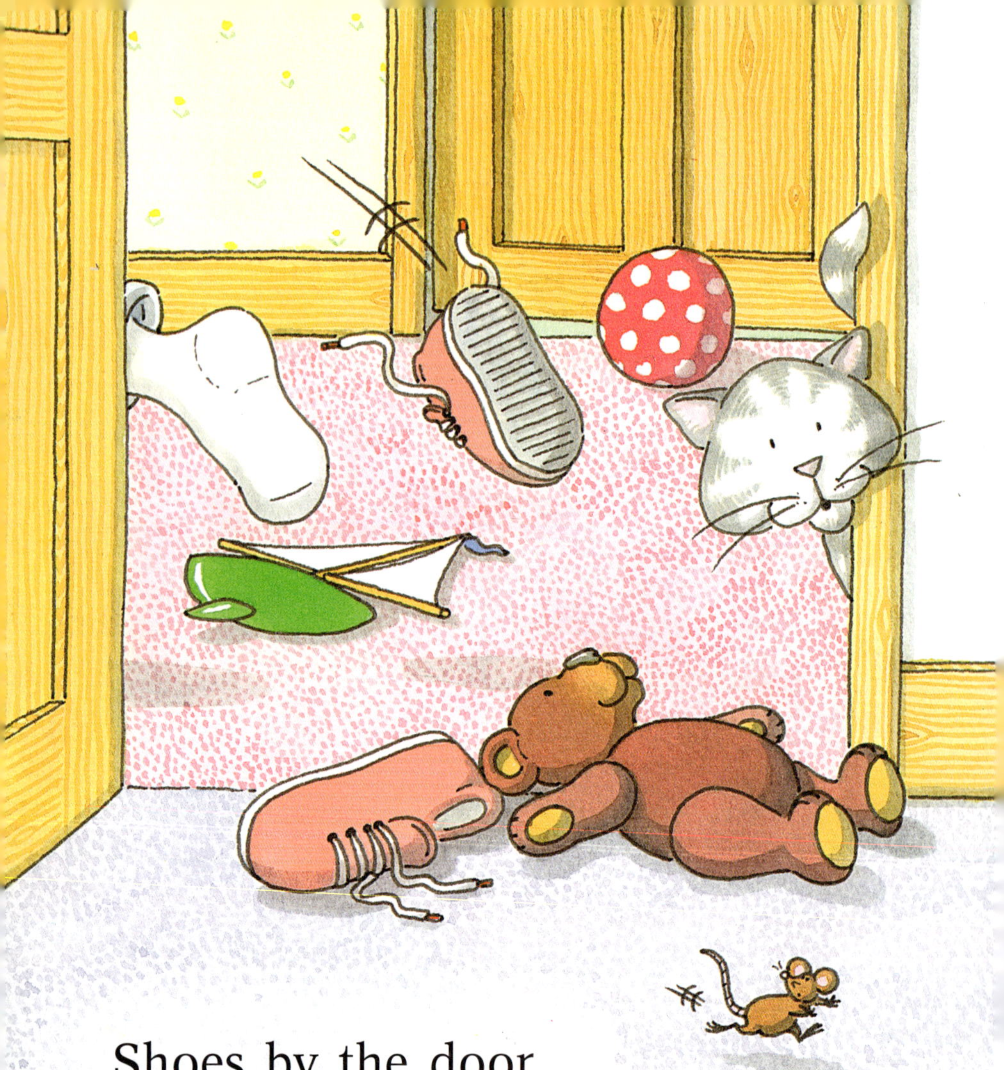

Shoes by the door.

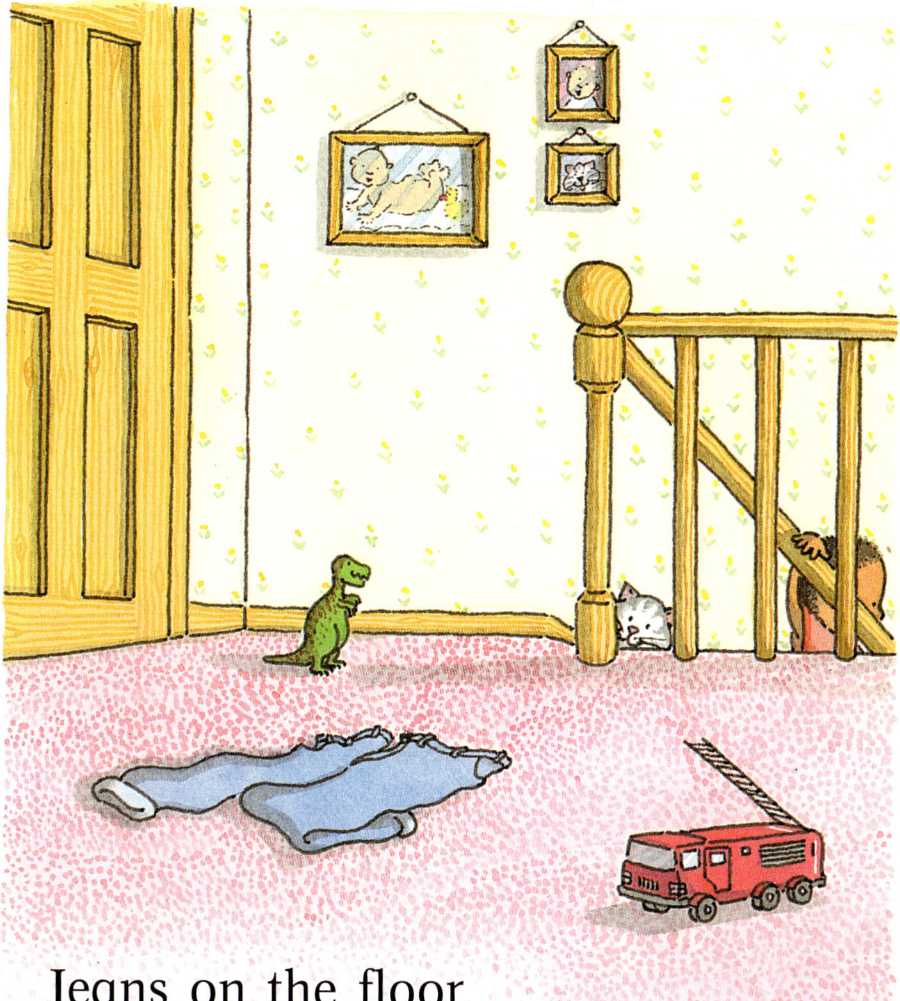

Jeans on the floor.

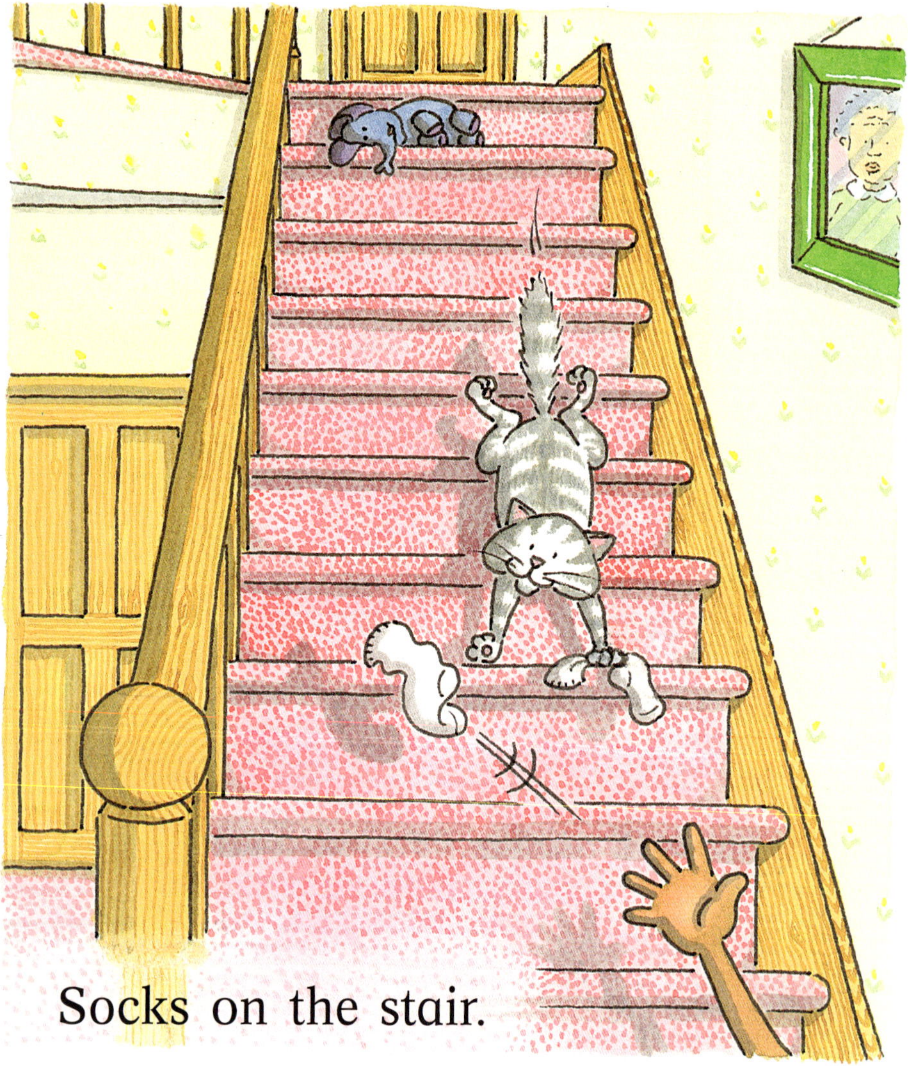

Socks on the stair.

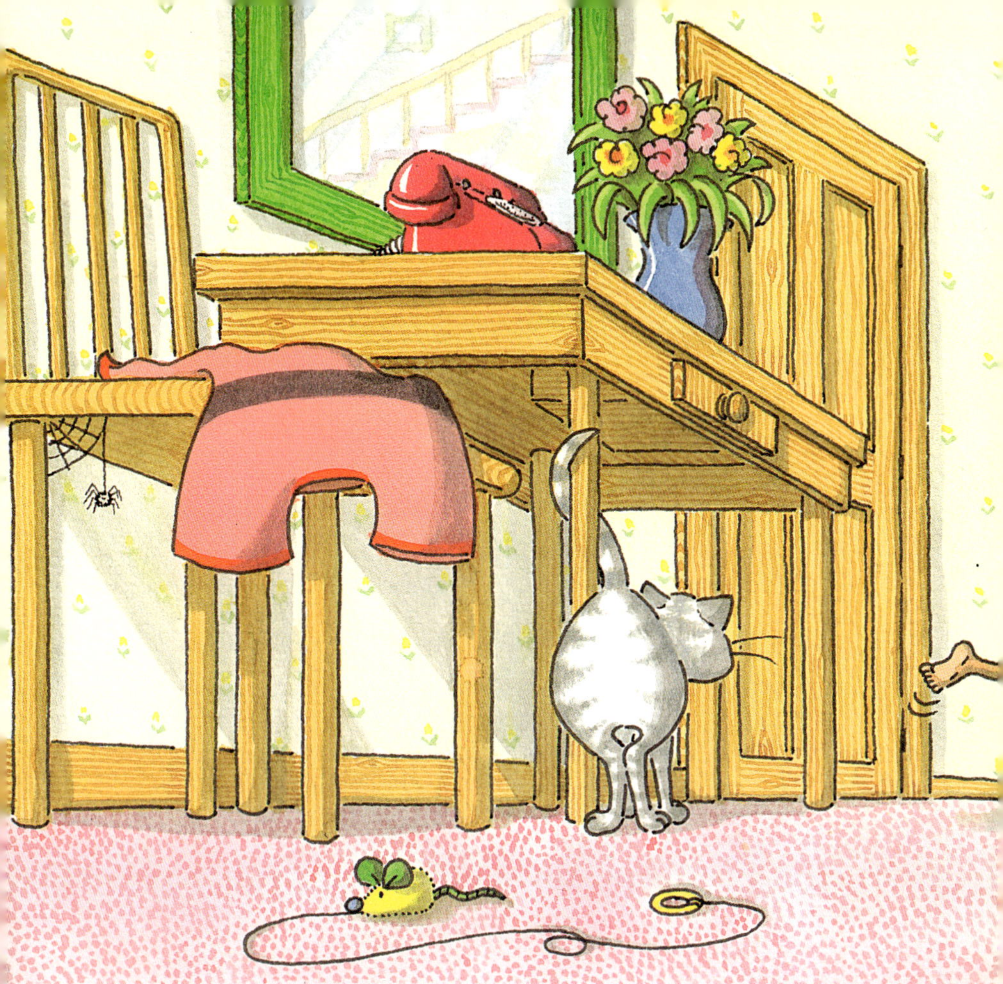

T-shirt on the chair.

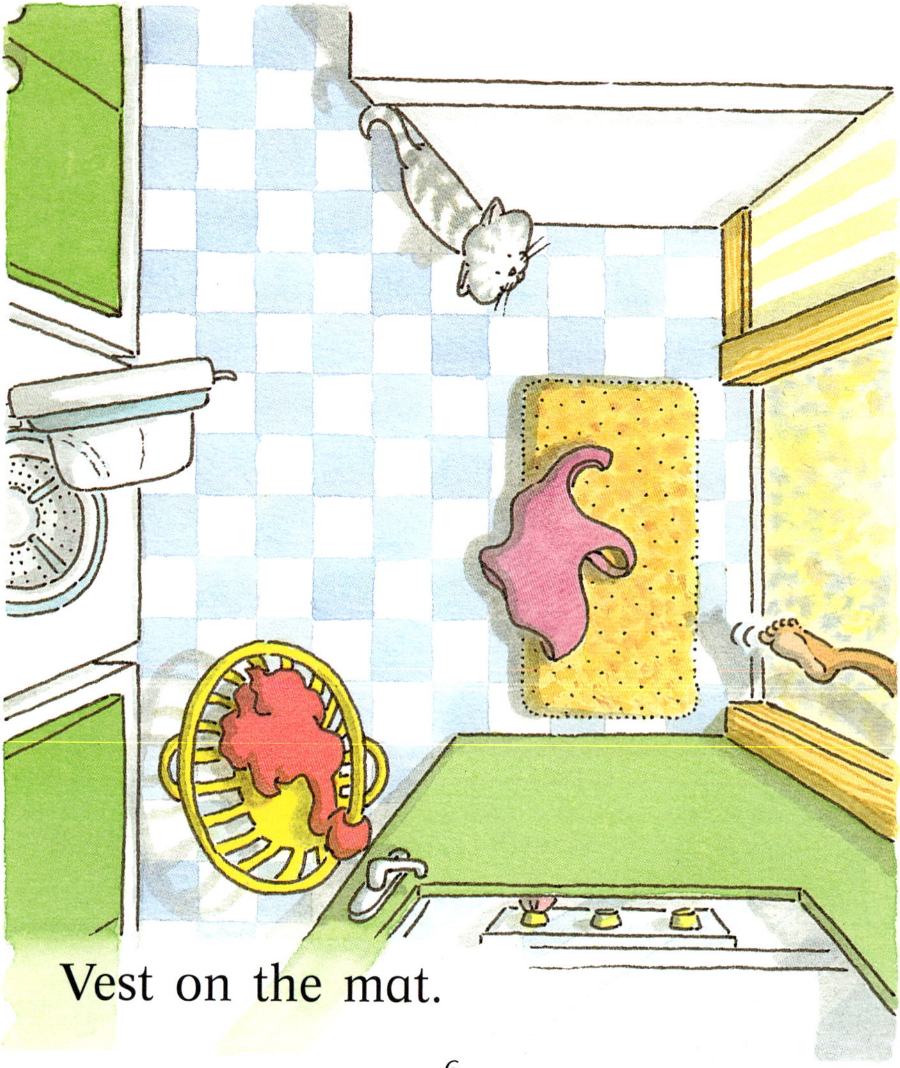

Vest on the mat.

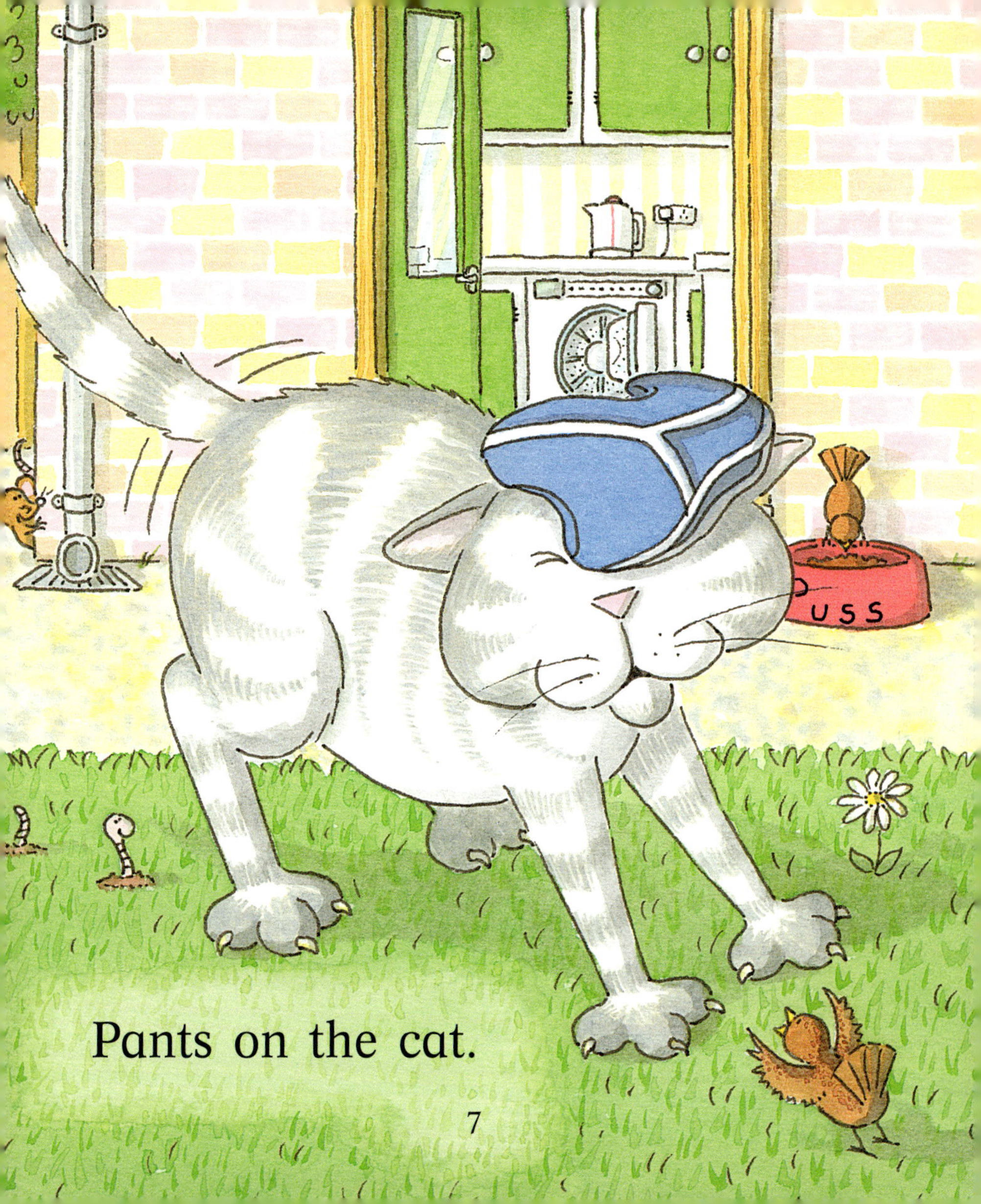

Pants on the cat.

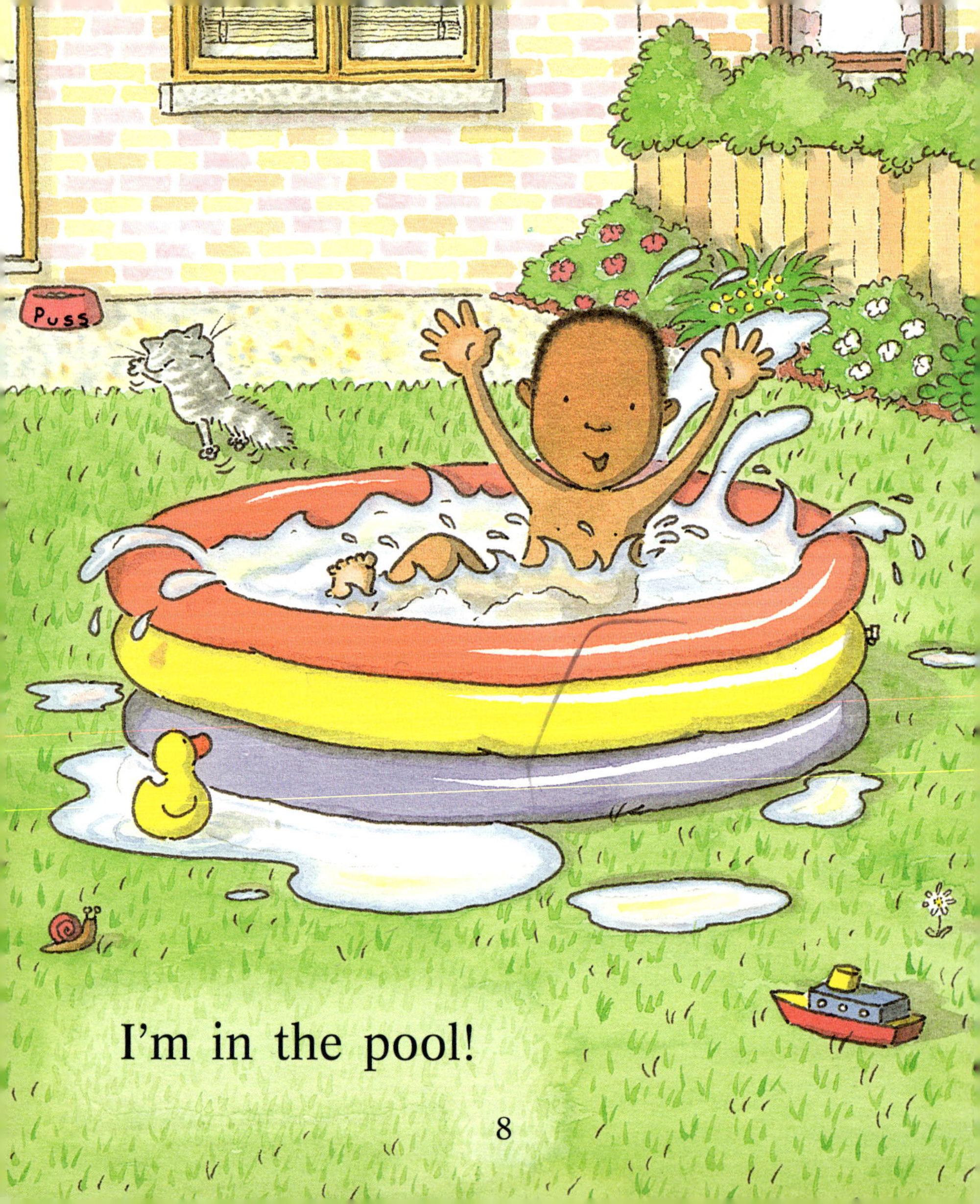


I'm in the pool!